HARD RAIN

HARD RAIN

A Chapbook

Tony Hoagland

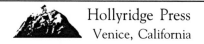
Hollyridge Press
Venice, California

Hollyridge Press
P.O. Box 2872
Venice, California 90294
www.hollyridgepress.com

Cover and Book Design by Rio Smyth
Cover Image by Jeff Gynane / Dreamstime.com
Author photo by Dorothy Alexander
Manufactured in the United States of America by Lightning Source

ISBN-13: 978-0-9772298-2-6
ISBN-10: 0-9772298-2-3

Grateful acknowledgment is made to the editors of the following
publications where these poems first appeared:

American Poetry Review: "Forty-Year Old Wine"; "Summer"; "Visitation"
Barrow Street: "Greed"
The Believer: "Hard Rain"
The Cincinnati Review: "A Quiet Town By The Sea"
Gulf Coast: "Dialectical Materialism"
Ploughshares: "Voyage"
Poetry: "Cement Truck"; "Hostess"; "Requests for Toy Piano"
Pool: "Breaking Up Is Hard To Do"
NightSun: "Responsibility in Metaphor"
Speakeasy: "Romantic Moment"; "And The Men"
Triquarterly: "Food Court"; "Allegory of the Temp Agency"

"Fire" appeared previously in *What Narcissism Means To Me (Graywolf, 2003)*

12 11 10 09 08 07 06   10 9 8 7 6 5 4 3 2

Contents

Hard Rain

FOODCOURT

If you want to talk about America, why not just mention
Jimmy's Wok and Roll American-Chinese Gourmet Emporium?—
the cloud of steam rising from the bean sprouts and shredded cabbage

when the oil is sprayed on from a giant plastic bottle
wielded by Ramon, Jimmy's main employee,
who hates having to wear the sanitary hair net

and who thinks the food smells funny?
And the secretaries from the law firm
                              drifting in from work at noon
to fill the tables of the foodcourt,
in their cotton skirts and oddly sexy running shoes?

Why not mention the little grove of palm trees
maintained by the mall corporation
and the splashing fountain beside it

and the faint smell of dope-smoke drifting from the men's room
where two boys from the suburbs
dropped off by their moms

with their baggy ghetto pants and skateboards
are getting ready to pronounce their first sentences
                              in African-American?

Oh yes, everything
all chopped up and stirred together
                              in the big steel pan
held over a medium-high blue flame

while Jimmy watches
with his practical black eyes.

FORTY-YEAR OLD WINE

On tv a guy named Franklin Meriwether is opening
a bottle of two-hundred dollar, forty-year old Bordeaux
to see if it's still good. "Something else
for the idiots to watch" says Shiela from the couch
but we all keep watching as he fills ten minutes
explaining the subtleties of cork extraction
and then ten minutes more to pour the dark blood-colored wine
into a glass shaped like a small breast.
"How much did it cost?" asks Ryan,
who just came into the room.
"Three hundred dollars," says Shiela, and Mike says, "Be quiet,"
as if there was something to hear
as the camera zooms in and we all grow silent
to watch the smallest muscles of Franklin's face
flicker with joy or disapproval
at the moment the wine steps onto his tongue
like a pilgrim entering the holy city
where the story ends
and the judgment begins.

RESPONSIBILITY IN METAPHOR

When I say she looked at me like a motel looking at a highway,
I mean the light was on above her parking lot.
I mean I could see the pink neon of the Vacancy sign
                                        all the way from the off-ramp.

I mean her lobby door was slightly open
and through the plate glass I could see
a roomkey hanging on one of those little brass hooks
                                behind the receptionist's desk.

When I say she looked at me like a motel looking at a highway,
I mean that in the quiet alcove of that glance,
            there was a Coke machine humming
                                    beside a tropical plant,

I could hear the *ding* of the elevator door
and from there it seemed an easy step to
            being transported swiftly upwards
to the second or third or even fourth floor of possibility.

I mean that walking down the carpeted hallway
I could hear, behind each door, a dripping faucet

And I could sense those little complimentary bars of soap
                                                beside the sink
telepathically requesting to have their wrappers removed—

That's what I mean when I say she looked at me
                                like a motel looking at a highway.

That may not be okay with you,

but remember, I'm just an ordinary highway—

my job is mostly holding steady
right between the lines, I go on and on,
I'm not a fairy tale or a sentimental journey.

All of my imagination goes to
getting here and there connected;

And after a long day of driving Me through Me,
I need a place to stop and rest,

And I don't mind a little small talk.

CEMENT TRUCK

I wanted to get the cement truck into the poem
because I loved the bulk of the big rotating barrel
        as it went calmly down the street,
churning to keep the wet cement inside
                    slushily in motion.

I liked the monster girth of the torso
                and the tilted ovoid shape,
the raised rump with a hole like an anus at the back,
the double-thick tires to bear the weight. I liked
        the way that people turned to watch it pass—

because what is more like a rhinoceros or elephant
than this thick-skinned grunting beast
        goaded by two smallish men in jumpsuits?
Taking its ponderous time to obey,
        drizzling a stream of juice between its legs?

I knew that I might have to make the center of the poem wider
when the cement truck had to turn a corner,
        scraping the bark of an overhanging tree,
giving a nudge to the power lines—

then having to turn around again, because
the drivers have somehow gotten lost:
one of them running to borrow a garden hose
                to wet down the load again,
one of them cursing and shaking out the map.

I liked the idea of my poem having room inside
for something as real as that truck
and having to get there by two o'clock or else
to pour the floor of the high school gymnasium.

—And I think at this point it would have been a terrible mistake
to turn the truck
into a metaphor or symbol for something else.
It had taken me so long to get the world into my poem,
and so long to get my poem into the world.

Now I didn't want to go back.
Now I had a four lane highway to drive down the middle of,
and a pair of black, heavy rubber boots,
and a mysterious rectangular lever just in front of the stick shift.
I wonder what that one does?

DIALECTICAL MATERIALISM

I was thinking about dialectical materialism at the supermarket,

strolling among the Chilean tomatoes and the Pilipino pineapples

admiring the Washington state apples stacked in perfect pyramid displays
by the ebony man from Zimbabwe wearing the Chicago Bulls t-shirt.

I was seeing the whole produce section
                              as a system of cross-referenced signifiers
   in a textbook of historical economics

and the fine spray that misted the vegetables
was like the cool mist of style imposed on meaning.

It was one of those days
when interpretation is brushing its varnish over everything

when even the birds are speaking complete sentences

and the sun is a brassy blond novelist of immense accomplishment
         dictating her new blockbuster
to a stenographer who types at the speed of light
and publishes each page as fast as it is written.

There was cornbread rising in the bakery department
and in its warm aroma I believed that I could smell
                              the exhaled breath of vanished Iroquois
their journey west and
                              delicate withdrawal into the forests

whereas by comparison
the coarse-grained wheat baguettes

seemed to irrepressibly exude
      the sturdy sweat and labor of eighteenth-century Europe.

My god there is so much sorrow in the grocery store!
You would have to be high
on the fumes of the piped-in pan flutes
                  of commodified Peruvian folk music

not to be driven practically driven crazy
with awe and shame,

not to weep at the scale of subjugated matter:

the ripped up etymologies of kiwi fruit and bratwurst,
the roads paved with dead languages
the jungles digested by foreign money.

It's the owners, I said to myself,
 it's the horrible juggernaut of progress

but the cilantro in my hand
opened up its bitter minty ampoule underneath my nose

and the bossa nova muzak charmed me like a hypnotist
and the pretty cashier with the shaved head and
            nose ring said *Have a nice day*

as I burst with my groceries through the automatic doors
into the open sky and air

but I was also in a giant parking lot
at a mega-mall outside of Minneapolis
                  where in row E 87
a Ford Escort from Mankato
            had just had a fender-bender with a Honda from Miami;

and these personified portions of my heart, the drivers
were standing there
in the gathering midwestern granular descending dusk

waiting for the trooper to fill out the accident report,

with the rotating red light of the squad car
                              whipping in circles above them
splashing their shopped-out middle-aged faces strangely
                              with war paint the hue of cherry Gatorade

and each of them was thinking
how with dialectical materialism, accidents happen:

how at any minute,
convenience can turn
                    into a kind of trouble you never wanted.

VISITATION

Now when I visit Ellen's body in my memory,
it is like visiting a cemetery. I look
at the chiseled, muscular belly
and at the perfect thirty-year old breasts
and the fine blond purse of her pussy
and I kneel and weep a little there.
I am not the first person to locate god
in erectile tissue and the lubricating gland
but when I kiss her breast and feel
the tough button of her nipple
rise and stiffen to my tongue
like the dome of a small mosque
in an ancient, politically-incorrect city,
I feel holy, I begin to understand religion.
I circle around to see the basilica
of her high, Irish-American butt,
and I look at her demure little asshole
and am sorry I didn't spend more time with it.
And her mouth and her eyes and white white teeth.
It's beauty beauty beauty which in a way Ellen
herself the person distracted me from. It's
beauty which has been redistributed now
by the justice of chance and the temporal economy.
Now I'm like a sad astronaut living
deep in space, breathing the oxygen of memory
out of a silver can. Now I'm like an angel
drifting over the surface of the earth,
brushing its meadows and forests
with the tips of my wings,
with wonder and regret and affection.

CONFINEMENT

The dictator in the turban died, and was replaced
by a dictator in a western business suit.
Now that he looked like all the other leaders, observers

detected a certain relaxing of tensions. Something in the air
suggested the weather was changing, in a slow, swirling
          rotation over the whole round globe.

Meanwhile we were driving
to my brother-in-law's funeral, running the yellow lights,
getting there late, taking our place in a line of cars

idling outside the cemetery. Nine in a row:
exhaust pouring out of the nine tailpipes
with an air of perfect patience. Having to wait because

no one had gotten the code number
to punch into the keypad on the automatic gate.
Cold day. The neighborhood, ugly and poor, like a runny nose,

and Barney was dead, big bad-habit Barney,
famous for his lack of self-control,
now needing an extra-large coffin,

as if he was taking his old friends
Drinking Eating and Smoking
into the hole with him.

—So what hovered over the proceedings that afternoon
was a mixture of grief and vindication.
He-wouldn't-listen-to-a-thing we said,

and now he's croaked, is what nobody said out loud,
but even so, you could read the text
in the pinched faces of the aunts,

or hear it being subsonically broadcast
by Vengeful Relative Radio.
Later, at the reception, I saw my beautiful ex-wife,

wearing her tight black dress,
standing beside a guy I would like to call her future
ex-boyfriend, gazing at a horrible painting on the wall.

A long time since she and I had been extinct,
but still I found inside myself a fierce desire
to go over and explain to them the six or seven

ways to recognize bad art.
And finally, the question seemed to be, for me:
Was the list of people I could love
exactly the same as the list
                              of people I could control?

Upstairs, looking for a place to be alone,
I found a television turned on and abandoned in a room,
sound off, churning light into the walls:

pictures of crowds, marching down streets, past
burning, overturned cars. Men dressed in nightgowns
gathered outside embassies, and throwing stones.

That was when I suddenly felt that I could understand
why they were protesting,
what they were so angry about:

They wanted to be let out of the TV set.
They had been trapped in there, and they wanted out.

ALLEGORY OF THE TEMP AGENCY

In the painting titled,
The Allegory of the Temp Agency,
the employers are depicted as wolves

with blood red mouths and yellow greedy eyes,
pursuing the small-business employees through the dark forest
of capitalism. It is night and

by the light of the minimum-wage moon we can see
the long pink tongues of the bosses hanging out
and the dilated white eyeballs of the employees as they flee

through woods, lacking any sense of
solidarity or collective organizing power.

Upon closer inspection the leaves beneath their feet
are shredded dollar bills which bear the distressed expressions
of ex-presidents and the wind in the trees is making a long

howl of no health insurance or job security
and No, it is not really a very good painting,
heavy handed in concept, and comic unintentionally in a way that

invites us to laugh at the desire for justice—
Rather, the painting shows that the artist was untalented,
and is an allegory of how difficult it is

to be both skillful and sincere
which in turn explains why the art
that hangs in the lobbies of banks

and in the boardrooms of corporate office buildings
is often made of black and white slashes
against a background of melted orange crayon

or glowing lavender rectangles floating in grey haze,
works in which no human figures appear,
in which the Haves

do not appear to be chatting and laughing
as they eat their sushi
carved from the lives of the Have-Nots.

REQUESTS FOR TOY PIANO

Play the one about the family of the ducks
where the ducks go down to the river
and one of them thinks the water will be cold
but then they jump in anyway
and like it and splash around.

No, I must play the one
about the nervous man from Palestine in row 14
with a brown bag in his lap
in which a gun is hidden in a sandwich.

Play the one about the handsome man and woman
standing on the steps of her apartment
and how the darkness and her perfume and the beating of their hearts
conjoin to make them feel
like leaping from the edge of chance—

No, I should play the one about
the hard rectangle of the credit card
hidden in the man's back pocket
and how the woman spent an hour
plucking out her brows, and how her perfume
was made from the destruction of a hundred flowers.

Then play the one about the flower industry
in which the migrant workers curse their own infected hands
from tossing sheaves of roses and carnations
into the back of the refrigerated trucks.

No, I must play the one about the single yellow daffodil
standing on my kitchen table
whose cut stem draws the water upwards
so the plant is flushed with the conviction

that the water has been sent
to find and raise it up
from somewhere so deep inside the earth
not even flowers can remember.

ROMANTIC MOMENT

After seeing the nature documentary we walk down Canyon Road,
into the plaza of art galleries and high end clothing stores

where the mock orange is fragrant in the summer night
and the smooth adobe walls glow fleshlike in the dark.

It is just our second date, and we sit down on a bench,
holding hands, not looking at each other,

and if I were a bull penguin right now I would lean over
and vomit softly into the mouth of my beloved

and if I were a peacock I'd flex my gluteal muscles to
erect and spread the quills of my cinemax tail.

If she were a female walkingstick bug she might
insert her hypodermic proboscis delicately into my neck

and inject me with a rich hormonal sedative
before attaching her egg sac to my thoracic undercarriage,

and if I were a young chimpanzee I would break off a nearby treelimb
and smash all the windows in the plaza jewelry stores.

And if she was a Brazilian leopard frog she would wrap her impressive
tongue three times around my right thigh and

pummel me lightly against the surface of our pond
and I would know her feelings were sincere.

Instead we sit awhile in silence, until
she remarks that in the relative context of tortoises and iguanas,

human males seem to be actually rather expressive.
And I say that female crocodiles really don't receive

enough credit for their gentleness.
Then she suggests that it is time for us to go

to get some ice cream cones and eat them.

SUMMER

God moves mysterious thunderheads over the towns and office buildings,
cracks them open like raw eggs. The north has critical humidity.
The south plucks at its sweaty clothes. The weatherman says it's August,
and a sniper is haunting Washington D.C.

He's picking victims at random from shopping malls and parking lots,
touching them with bullets like blue fingertips,

and some say he's an unemployed geek with a chip on his shoulder,
and some say he's an agent of ancient Greek theology.

Gibb says the sniper is a surrealist travel agent
                                        booking departures only
Or he's a dada lawyer without a client
                                        arguing in thirty caliber sentences.

Robin says the sniper is what the country invented
                                        as a symptom of its mental illness
and Marcia is sad because she knows the sniper could have been cured
by a regimen of vitamins and serotonin reuptake inhibitors.

We had fallen into one of our periodic comas
                                        of obesity and celebrity
when the sniper went off like an alarm clock

and the preacher on TV
said that he had come according to Revelations 3:14
to punish us for the crime of not being ready for death—

but as Snoopy the clerk at the 7-11 said,
What kind of crime is that?

Meanwhile the air conditioners are working overtime,
the rooftops are full of swat teams and camera crews
and the sky too is mobilizing:
dark clouds without speaking; menacing millennial clouds.

We don't know yet what the metaphysical facts are;
We don't know if our sniper is domestic or foreign terror,
what color the chip on his shoulder is
or what we will do if the sniper chooses us tomorrow.

But when we go out now, we feel our nakedness.
Each step has a slender string attached.
And when we move, we move more quietly,
as we slide between the sinners and the snipers

and the summer,
in the simmering medicinal rain.

HOSTESS

All I remember from that party
is the little black dress of our hostess
held up by nothing more
than a shoestring of raw silk

which kept slipping off her shoulder
—So the whole time she was talking to you
about real estate or vinaigrette,

you would watch it gradually
slide down her creamy arm
until the very last moment
when she shrugged it back in place again.

Oh the business of that dress
was non-specific and unspeakable,
and it troubled all of us

like the boundary of a disputed territory
or the edge of a borderline personality.
It was like a story you wanted to see
brought to a conclusion, but

it was also like a story stuck
in the middle of itself, as it kept on
almost happening, but not,
then almost happening again—

It took all night for me to understand
the dress was designed to fail like that;
the hostess was designed to keep it up,
as we were designated to chew

the small rectangles of food
they serve at such affairs, and to salivate
while the night moved us around in its mouth.

This is the way in which parties
are dreamlike, duplicitous places
where you hang in a kind of suspense
between the real and the pretended.

All I remember from that night
is that I had come for a mysterious reason,
which I waited to see revealed.

And that, by the end of the evening,
I had found my disappointment,
which I hoped no one else had seen.

OPERATIONS

In autumn, Operation Enduring Freedom commenced,
which some party-poopers wanted to nickname Operation Infinite
    Self-Indulgence.
We tied flags to the antennae of our cars
that snapped like fire when we drove.

In winter there was Operation Gentle Sledgehammer,
which seemed linguistically a little underdigested,
but we lined up squads of second-graders
               to stand at attention while we beat a drum.

Let me make it clear that I was
as doubtful as anyone about Operation Racial Provocation
but I loved Operation Religious Suspicion,

which led to Operation Eye For An Eye,
which was succeeded by Operation Helping Hand;
—Let me tell you that was a scary-looking hand!
But that was also a very successful Operation.

Someday you will be required to perform a terrible deed
in order to save yourself,
                  but save yourself for what?

That would be a question for Operation
Self-Examination to answer,
which is a very painful operation
performed without anesthesia
in a naked room full of shadows and light.

Perhaps I might suggest, instead,
Operation Self-Medication, or Operation Endless Mindless Distraction?
In the meantime Operation Collateral Amnesia
is proceeding very smoothly.
When it is over we want call it Operation One Big Happy Family—
Is that okay with you?

FIRE

The rock band set off fireworks as part of their show—
the ceiling tile of the nightclub smoldered and flared up
over the heads of all those dancing bodies below—

Then they churned and burned against the exit doors,
doors someone had chained shut to prevent the would-be sneakers-in—
So 95 party people died that night,

and two days later at the televised funeral the weeping girl
says of her dead friend David,
"God must have needed some good rock and roll in heaven."

On earth, God must have needed some good clichés, too,
and weeping riot girls with runny mascara and spiderweb tattoos.
He must have needed the entertainment of dueling insurance companies

calculating the liability per body bag
and the rock band and nightclub owner pointing fingers at each
    other like guns
and pulling the blame-trigger, *blam blam blam*

because death is something that always has to be enclosed
by an elaborate set of explanations.
It is an ancient litigation,

this turning of horror into stories,
and it is a lonely piece of work,
trying to turn the stories back into horror,

but somebody has to do it
—especially now that God
has reverted to a state of fire.

IN A QUIET TOWN BY THE SEA

Once I listened to two guys talk about screwing around.
One of them said he liked to meet someone
in a city far away from where he lived
and to get her into the crisp white sheets of a hotel bed.

He said skin was the holiest testament of all
and that to remove the clothes of a sexualized stranger
was like filling your lungs with oxygen
before diving into the swimming pool of god.

He said, Pleasure doesn't care
        whose cup you drink it from—

and you could tell it was something he had read once in a book,
written down and practiced in his head.

The other guy said that the stink from secrets in a marriage
was like the smell of decomposing flesh

rising from under the foundation of your house.
He said love is writing your name in cement,

and anyway his wife would know in a NASCAR minute
if he came home with the smell of pussy on his clothes.

There were drinks on the table of course
and a blonde waitress buzzing around
        like the goddess of temptation in a budget film
whose breasts, silhouetted in her blouse,

were like exhibits A and B in the impending criminal case
as she herself was clearly
destined to be evidence
         for both the defense and prosecution.

And there was something so typical about these guys
with their alcohol and their forgetting,

their longing to conquer the world
and yet to still be coddled by their mommy-wives,

you wanted to have them dipped in plastic for a keychain,
or to turn to the salesman and say,
Can we see something a little, no, please, something *completely* different?

Outside the moon gazed upon the earth with wary ardor;
the church cast its shadow upon the plaza
like a triangle and square
         in a troubling geometry problem.

and in the houses and the neighborhoods,
it's distressing to report,
there was no one sleeping. There was no one sleeping

who did not dream of being touched.

AND THE MEN

want back in:
all the Dougs and the Michaels, the Darnells, the Erics and Josés,
they're standing by the off-ramp of the interstate
holding up cardboard signs that say *WILL WORK FOR RELATIONSHIP.*

Their love-mobiles are rusty.
Their Shaggin' Wagons are up on cinderblocks.
They're reading self-help books and practicing abstinence,
taking out Personals ads that say
        "Good listener would like to meet lesbian ladies,
                for purposes of friendship only."

In short, they've changed their minds, the men:
they want another shot at the collaborative enterprise.
Want to do fifty-fifty housework and childcare;
They want commitment renewal weekends and couples therapy.

Because being a man was finally too sad—
In spite of the perks, the lifetime membership benefits.
And it got old,
telling the joke about the hooker and the priest

at the company barbeque, praising the vintage of the beer and
        punching the shoulders of a bud
            in a little overflow of homosocial bonhomie—
Always holding the fear inside
            like a tipsy glass of water—

Now they're ready to talk, really talk about their feelings,
in fact they're ready to make you sick with revelations of
            their vulnerability—
A pool of testosterone is spreading from around their feet,

it's draining out of them like radiator fluid,
like history, like an experiment that failed.

So here they come on their hands and knees, the men:
Here they come. They're really beaten. No tricks this time.
       No fine print.
Please, they're begging you. Look out.

BREAKING UP IS HARD TO DO

On Friday afternoon David said he was divesting his holdings
        in Stephanie dot org.
And Cindy announced she was getting rid of all her Dan-obelia,
        and did anyone want a tennis racket or a cardigan?

Alice told Michael that she was transplanting herself
        to another brand of potting soil
And Jason composed a 3-chord blues song called
        "I Can't Rake Your Leaves Anymore Mama,"
then insisted on playing it
        over his speakerphone to Ellen.

The moon rose up in the western sky
        with an expression of complete exhaustion,
like a 38-year old single mother
        standing at the edge of the playground. Right at that moment

Betty was extracting coil after coil of Andrew's
        emotional intestines
        through a verbal incision she had made in his heart,
and Jane was parachuting into an Ani Difranco concert
        wearing a banner saying, *Get Lost, Mark Resnick.*

That's how you find out:
out of the blue.
And it hurts, baby, it really hurts,
because breaking up is hard to do.

GREED

painted on a wall on 20th and Grant—just the word,
Greed. Just that word facing the street
for the drivers in their cars to read
while waiting for the light to change.

No who, no why, or is, just *Greed*
with no appendage—no promised consequence;
not greed as deadly sin, or greed named
as a traditional form of suffering.

What is surprising is that, after all the words
that have been chiseled into us,
—stenciled, scrawled, printed and embossed,
we still seem able to read one more.

Just the word *Greed*, at eye level,
printed on the wall at Grant and 20th.
Greed, said calmly, without inflection.

TO REMEMBER HISTORY YOU
HAVE TO REPEAT IT

The woman newscaster with the beautiful voice
is talking about the surface-to-air missiles:
What has she done to her hair? asks someone

and the flare and combustion on the screen behind her
is an orange haze against which her face is calm and clear.
She cut it back, says someone else, glancing at the menu,
raising a hand to get the waiter's attention—

The suicide bombers, they pass through her going one way,
and the funerals pass through going back the other;
The refugees are waiting at her border
like puppies waiting for adoption, the petroleum spill

gushes from her mouth, right before our eyes, but
she never cries or laughs or mispronounces.
I can imagine her going home, heating up

spaghetti from a can, telling her husband she's too tired tonight
—No wonder. She handles the hot sectors and razor wire.
She makes the failure of negotiations all right.

If I sneaked into her house tonight, if I went into her bedroom
and pressed my ear against her stomach, I believe that I could hear
troop movements and weather reports, staticky cries
of dying men, torn ligaments of this enormous body—

To remember history you have to repeat it and she does.
We stand around her like children and listen.
We stand around her like wild beasts disguised as children.

THE SPACE PROGRAM

In the history of American speech,
he was born between "Dirty commies" and "Nice tits."

He worked for Uncle Sam,
and married a dizzy gal from Pittsburgh with a mouth on her.

I was conceived in the decade
between "Far out" and "Whatever;"

at the precise moment when "going all the way"
turned into "getting it on."

Sometimes, I swear I can feel the idiom flying around inside my head
like moths leftover from the age of Aquarius

or I hear myself speak and it feels like I am wearing
a no-longer-groovy cologne from the Seventies.

In those days I was always trying to get a real rap session going
and he was always telling me how to clean out the garage.

Our last visit took place in the twilight zone
between "feeling no pain" and "catching a buzz."

For that occasion I had carefully prepared
a suitcase full of small talk

—but he was already packed and going backwards,
with the nice tits and the dirty commies,

to the small town of his vocabulary,
somewhere outside of Pittsburgh.

HARD RAIN

After I heard *It's a Hard Rain's A-Gonna Fall*
played softly by an accordion quartet
through the ceiling speakers at the Springdale Shopping Mall,
I understood there's nothing
we can't pluck the stinger from,

nothing we can't turn into a soft drink flavor or a t-shirt.
Even serenity can become something horrible
if you make a commercial about it
using smiling, white-haired people

quoting Thoreau to sell retirement homes
in the Everglades, where the swamp has been
drained and bulldozed into a nineteen-hole golf course
with electrified alligator barriers.

You can't keep beating yourself up, Billy
I heard the therapist say on television
                                        to the teenage murderer,
About all those people you killed—
You just have to be the best person you can be,

one day at a time—

and everybody in the audience claps and weeps a little,
because the level of deep feeling has been touched,
and they want to believe that
the power of Forgiveness is greater
than the power of Consequence, or History.

Dear Abby:
My father is a businessman who travels.
Each time he returns from one of his trips,
his shoes and trousers
                    are covered with blood—
but he never forgets to bring me a nice present;
Should I say something?
                    Signed, America.

I used to think I was not part of this,
that I could mind my own business and get along,

but that was just another song
that had been taught to me since birth—

whose words I was humming under my breath,
as I was walking thorough the Springdale Mall.

VOYAGE

I feel as if we opened a book about great ocean voyages
and found ourselves on a great ocean voyage:
sailing through December, around the horn of Christmas
and into the January Sea, and sailing on and on

in a novel without a moral but one in which
all the characters who died in the middle chapters
make the sunsets near the book's end more beautiful.

—And someone is spreading a map upon a table,
and someone is hanging a lantern from the stern,
and someone else says, "I'm only sorry
that I forgot my blue parka; It's turning cold."

Sunset like a burning wagon train
Sunrise like a dish of cantaloupe
Clouds like two armies clashing in the sky;
Icebergs and tropical storms,
That's the kind of thing that happens on our ocean voyage—

And in one of the chapters I was blinded by love
And in another, anger made us sick like swallowed glass
& I lay in my bunk and slept for so long,

I forgot about the ocean,
Which all the time was going by, right there, outside my cabin window.

And the sides of the ship were green as money,
and the water made a sound like memory when we sailed.

Then it was summer. Under the constellation of the swan,
under the constellation of the horse.

At night we consoled ourselves
By discussing the meaning of homesickness.
But there was no home to go home to.
There was no getting around the ocean.
We had to go on finding out the story
                              by pushing into it—

The sea was no longer a metaphor.
The book was no longer a book.
That *was* the plot.
That was our marvelous punishment.

Breinigsville, PA USA
29 December 2010
252367BV00003B/365/A